AIRPLANES from Then to Now

BY RACHEL GRACK

I0876361

SEQUENCE

AMICUS | AMICUS INK

Sequence is published by Amicus and Amicus Ink
P.O. Box 227, Mankato, MN 56002
www.amicuspublishing.us

Copyright © 2022 Amicus. International copyright reserved in all countries. No part of this book may be reproduced in any form without written permission from the publisher.

Library of Congress Cataloging-in-Publication Data
Names: Koestler-Grack, Rachel A., 1973- author. | Koestler-Grack, Rachel A., 1973-Developments in technology.
Title: Airplanes from then to now / by Rachel Grack.
Description: Mankato, MN : Amicus/Amicus Ink, [2022] | Series: Sequence. Developments in technology | Includes bibliographical references and index. | Audience: Ages 7-10 | Audience: Grades 2-3 | Summary: "Full-color photographs and a running timeline illustrate important developments in aviation history. Topics feature gliders, the Wright Brothers and powered flight, multi-engine aircraft, passenger jets, supersonic aircraft, and drones. A table of contents, glossary, further resources, and an index are included"-- Provided by publisher.
Identifiers: LCCN 2019036335 (print) | LCCN 2019036336 (ebook) | ISBN 9781681519593 (library binding) | ISBN 9781681526065 (paperback) | ISBN 9781645490449 (pdf)
Subjects: LCSH: Airplanes--History--Juvenile literature. | Flight--History--Juvenile literature. | LCGFT: Instructional and educational works.
Classification: LCC TL547 .K66 2022 (print) | LCC TL547 (ebook) | DDC 629.133/3409--dc23
LC record available at https://lccn.loc.gov/2019036335
LC ebook record available at https://lccn.loc.gov/2019036336

Editor: Gillia Olson
Designer: Aubrey Harper
Photo Researcher: Bridget Prehn

Photo Credits: Aerion cover; Alamy / Andy Myatt 20–21, Chronicle 4–5, Justin Kase zninez 22–23, PA Images 16–17, Pictures Now 10–11; Boeing Images 19; Boom Supersonic 28–29; Getty / Handout 24, Underwood Archives 12; iStock/KOHb circuit texture (throughout); Newscom / Reuters / LEONHARD FOEGER 26–27; Science Source / Detlev van Ravenswaay 14; Wikimedia / Library of Congress 6–7; Flickr / San Diego Air and Space Museum Archive 8–9

TABLE OF CONTENTS

Lilienthal flies one of his gliders in Germany in 1894.

Otto Lilienthal tests his first successful glider.

1891

. . LOADING . . . LOADING

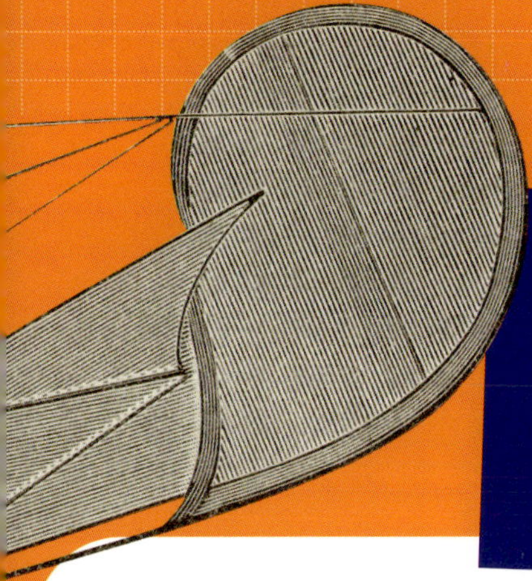

The First Flights

Long ago, people envied that birds could fly. People dreamed of traveling by air, too. Early inventors studied bird wings for ideas. The wing's shape matters. The way air moves over the wings helps birds fly. In 1891, Otto Lilienthal built a **glider**. It had huge, birdlike wings. He took the first real flight.

ADING . . . LOADING . . . LOADING . . .

To take off, gliders had to move fast. Gaining speed was hard without an engine. Orville and Wilbur Wright built a gas-powered engine. They tried many times to get it to fly. In 1903, they tested it near Kitty Hawk, North Carolina. Its spinning **propeller** lifted the plane off the ground. It flew 120 feet (37 m). This was the first powered airplane flight!

Orville Wright successfully flew the *Wright Flyer* for 12 seconds in 1903.

Otto Lilienthal tests his first successful glider.

1891

1903

LOADING . . . LOADING

The Wright brothers fly the first gas-powered airplane.

OADING . . . LOADING . . . LOADING . . .

Otto Lilienthal tests his first successful glider.

Igor Sikorsky builds the first multi-engine plane.

1891 | 1903 | 1913

G . . . LOADING

The Wright brothers fly the first gas-powered airplane.

Building Better Planes

The Wright brothers proved air travel was possible. But single-engine airplanes could only carry light loads. What about a plane to carry a group of people? In 1913, Igor Sikorsky built a four-engine plane. Each long wing carried two powerful engines. The engines lifted the plane's big, heavy **cabin** easily. Up to seven people could ride.

Sikorsky (right) built a plane to carry up to seven people in 1913.

LOADING . . . LOADING . . . LOADING . . .

Larger planes needed long **runways** to lift off. Most runways were short. Sikorsky designed another airplane—a flying boat. The *American Clipper* took off and landed on water. Open water provided a huge runway. The clipper flew its first passengers in 1931. Clippers could also travel across the ocean in one trip.

The *American Clipper* was a flying boat. It took off and landed on water.

- 1891: Otto Lilienthal tests his first successful glider.
- 1903: The Wright brothers fly the first gas-powered airplane.
- 1913: Igor Sikorsky builds the first multi-engine plane.
- 1931: The *American Clipper* flying boat takes its first flight.

LOADING

OADING . . . LOADING . . . LOADING . . .

The Stratoliner kept passengers comfortable at high altitudes.

- **1891** — Otto Lilienthal tests his first successful glider.
- **1903** — The Wright brothers fly the first gas-powered airplane.
- **1913** — Igor Sikorsky builds the first multi-engine plane.
- **1931** — The *American Clipper* flying boat takes its first flight.
- **1940** — Boeing flies the first high-altitude passenger airplane, the Stratoliner.

Clippers were low-flying planes. The weather could be rough. Air gets thinner at high **altitudes**. Thin air offers a nice, smooth flight. But people can't breathe well above 12,500 feet (3,810 m). In 1940, Boeing flew the first passenger plane with controlled **cabin pressure**. People could breathe at higher altitudes. The Stratoliner flew higher than previous planes.

- **1891** Otto Lilienthal tests his first successful glider.
- **1903** The Wright brothers fly the first gas-powered airplane.
- **1913** Igor Sikorsky builds the first multi-engine plane.
- **1931** The *American Clipper* flying boat takes its first flight.
- **1940** Boeing flies the first high-altitude passenger airplane, the Stratoliner.
- **1947** The Bell X-1 jet flies faster than the speed of sound.

Jets

Meanwhile, engineers were building faster airplanes. **Jet** engines give planes a stronger push. They use kerosene for fuel instead of gas. In 1947, the Bell X-1 was the first airplane to fly faster than the speed of sound. It reached the **supersonic** speed of 700 mph (1,127 km/h).

Chuck Yaeger flew the Bell X-1 on its first supersonic flight.

LOADING . . . LOADING . . . LOADING . . .

The first jets were mostly military planes. Geoffrey de Havilland designed the first passenger jet. In 1952, the Comet jetliner took its first passenger flight. Its sleek silver wings carried four turbojet engines. It flew higher, faster, and smoother than any other passenger plane. It carried 36 passengers. A new age of travel began!

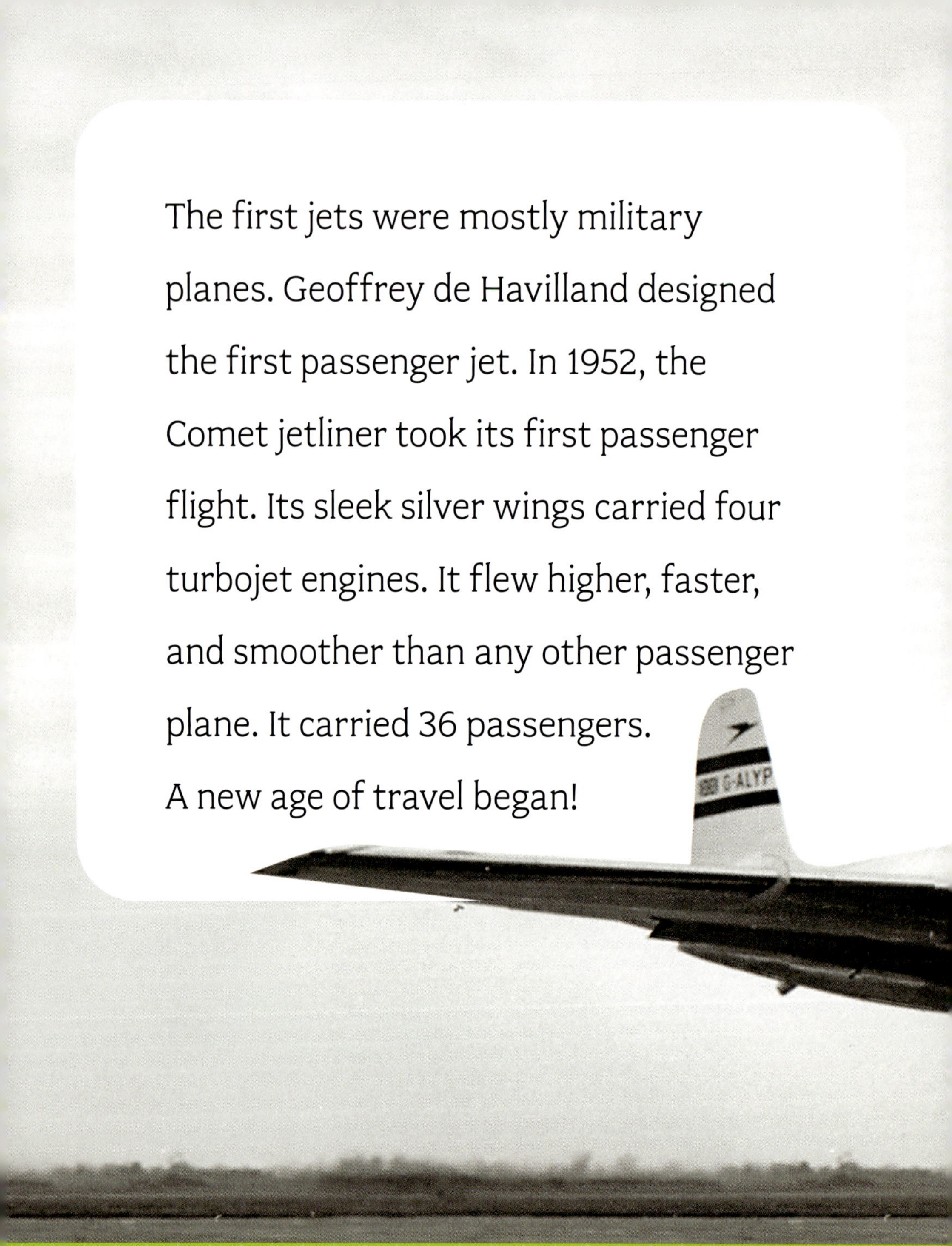

1891 — Otto Lilienthal tests his first successful glider.

1903 — The Wright brothers fly the first gas-powered airplane.

1913 — Igor Sikorsky builds the first multi-engine plane.

1931 — The *American Clipper* flying boat takes its first flight.

1940 — Boeing flies the first high-altitude passenger airplane, the Stratoliner.

1947 — The Bell X-1 jet flies faster than the speed of sound.

The Comet takes off from London, England, for its first flight in 1952.

1952

LOADING . . . LOADING . . .

The Comet jet airliner takes its first passenger flight.

The Age of Air Travel

Jets soon rumbled across the sky every day. But tickets were costly. Boeing wanted to make air travel cheaper. In 1969, it built a jumbo jet called the 747. Its engines ran on less fuel. Ticket prices came down. Each flight could carry more than 370 people. More people started to travel by plane.

1891 — Otto Lilienthal tests his first successful glider.

1903 — The Wright brothers fly the first gas-powered airplane.

1913 — Igor Sikorsky builds the first multi-engine plane.

1931 — The *American Clipper* flying boat takes its first flight.

1940 — Boeing flies the first high-altitude passenger airplane, the Stratoliner.

1947 — The Bell X-1 jet flies faster than the speed of sound.

Flight attendants pose with the new Boeing 747 at its launch.

The Boeing 747 makes flying less costly.

1952 1969

ING . . . LOADING . . .

The Comet jet airliner takes its first passenger flight.

1891 — Otto Lilienthal tests his first successful glider.

1903 — The Wright brothers fly the first gas-powered airplane.

1913 — Igor Sikorsky builds the first multi-engine plane.

1931 — The *American Clipper* flying boat takes its first flight.

1940 — Boeing flies the first high-altitude passenger airplane, the Stratoliner.

1947 — The Bell X-1 jet flies faster than the speed of sound.

Other jetliners focused on speed. In 1976, Concorde made the first supersonic passenger flight. A trip from London, England, to New York took only 3.5 hours. That was half the time of regular jetliners. But a ticket could cost $12,000. Most travelers took cheaper flights. Concorde stopped running in 2003.

The Concorde was super fast and super expensive.

1952 — The Comet jet airliner takes its first passenger flight.

1969 — The Boeing 747 makes flying less costly.

1976 — Concorde takes the first supersonic passenger flight.

. . . LOADING . . .

On short or long flights, passengers had ways to pass the time. They enjoyed meals, drinks, and maybe a movie. Modern technology pushed service to new heights. By 1991, Virgin airlines had seatback screens in all planes. Each passenger could choose what to watch. Today, many flights offer wireless streaming and internet.

Seatback screens, shown here on a Virgin airlines flight in 2009, gave customers entertainment options.

1891	Otto Lilienthal tests his first successful glider.
1903	The Wright brothers fly the first gas-powered airplane.
1913	Igor Sikorsky builds the first multi-engine plane.
1931	The *American Clipper* flying boat takes its first flight.
1940	Boeing flies the first high-altitude passenger airplane, the Stratoliner.
1947	The Bell X-1 jet flies faster than the speed of sound.

1952
The Comet jet airliner takes its first passenger flight.

1969
The Boeing 747 makes flying less costly.

1976
Concorde takes the first supersonic passenger flight.

1991
Virgin Airlines has seatback screens in all planes.

ADING . . .

Solar Impulse 2 flies over San Francisco after its flight across the Pacific Ocean in 2016.

- 1891 — Otto Lilienthal tests his first successful glider.
- 1903 — The Wright brothers fly the first gas-powered airplane.
- 1913 — Igor Sikorsky builds the first multi-engine plane.
- 1931 — The *American Clipper* flying boat takes its first flight.
- 1940 — Boeing flies the first high-altitude passenger airplane, the Stratoliner.
- 1947 — The Bell X-1 jet flies faster than the speed of sound.

Into the Future!

Engineers are testing new types of engines. In 2016, the first **solar** plane circled the world. *Solar Impulse 2* used only solar power. The 17,000 solar cells on its wings turn sunlight into engine power. Zunum is working on an airplane that uses both electricity and jet fuel.

1952 — The Comet jet airliner takes its first passenger flight.

1969 — The Boeing 747 makes flying less costly.

1976 — Concorde takes the first supersonic passenger flight.

1991 — Virgin Airlines has seatback screens in all planes.

2016 — *Solar Impulse 2* flies around the world without fuel power.

Would you ride a self-flying taxi? In 2019, a **drone** picked up its first rider in Vienna, Austria. This small, two-person plane is made for short trips. No pilot needed! These planes could work well for sudden medical problems. Traffic won't slow them down.

People take a test flight of a drone taxi in 2019.

1891 — Otto Lilienthal tests his first successful glider.

1903 — The Wright brothers fly the first gas-powered airplane.

1913 — Igor Sikorsky builds the first multi-engine plane.

1931 — The *American Clipper* flying boat takes its first flight.

1940 — Boeing flies the first high-altitude passenger airplane, the Stratoliner.

1947 — The Bell X-1 jet flies faster than the speed of sound.

- **1952** The Comet jet airliner takes its first passenger flight.
- **1969** The Boeing 747 makes flying less costly.
- **1976** Concorde takes the first supersonic passenger flight.
- **1991** Virgin Airlines has seatback screens in all planes.
- **2016** *Solar Impulse 2* flies around the world without fuel power.
- **2019** Self-flying taxi cabs are tested in Austria.

1891	1903	1913	1931	1940	1947
Otto Lilienthal tests his first successful glider.	The Wright brothers fly the first gas-powered airplane.	Igor Sikorsky builds the first multi-engine plane.	The *American Clipper* flying boat takes its first flight.	Boeing flies the first high-altitude passenger airplane, the Stratoliner.	The Bell X-1 jet flies faster than the speed of sound.

Airplanes streak overhead day and night. It's a common way to travel. What's next? Airplanes might fly at rocket speed. Companies are testing **hypersonic** jets. These airplanes could fly 3,000 mph (4,828 km/h)! A 15-hour flight would take 2 hours. Planes have come a long way since the first gliders. Perhaps birds now envy people's ability to fly!

The goal of Boom Supersonic's Overture plane is to travel faster than the Concorde but cost much less.

- 1952: The Comet jet airliner takes its first passenger flight.
- 1969: The Boeing 747 makes flying less costly.
- 1976: Concorde takes the first supersonic passenger flight.
- 1991: Virgin Airlines has seatback screens in all planes.
- 2016: *Solar Impulse 2* flies around the world without fuel power.
- 2019: Self-flying taxi cabs are tested in Austria.

Glossary

altitude Distance above the ground.

cabin A room within a plane, usually where passengers sit.

cabin pressure The measure of density of air within a plane.

drone An aircraft with no pilot.

glider An aircraft without an engine.

hypersonic Moving five times faster than the speed of sound.

jet An airplane powered by a jet engine.

propeller A set of spinning blades that push air backward and move a plane forward.

runway A strip of ground where aircraft take off and land.

solar Relating to the sun; solar cells turn sunlight into energy to create power.

supersonic Moving faster than the speed of sound.

Read More

DK Publishing. *Big Book of Airplanes.* New York: DK Publishing, 2016.

Lanier, Wendy Hinote. *Passenger Planes.* Lake Elmo, Minn.: Focus Readers, 2019.

Olson, Elsie. *Drones.* Modern Engineering Marvels. Minneapolis: Checkerboard Library, an imprint of Abdo Publishing, 2018.

Websites

DK Find Out! History of Aircraft

www.dkfindout.com/us/transportation/history-aircraft

National Geographic Kids: Taking Flight with the Wright Brothers

https://kids.nationalgeographic.com/explore/history/wright-brothers

PBS: Airport Field Trip

https://video.wpbt2.org/video/airport-wqeijh

Every effort has been made to ensure that these websites are appropriate for children. However, because of the nature of the Internet, it is impossible to guarantee that these sites will remain active indefinitely or that their contents will not be altered.

Index

About the Author

Rachel Grack has worked in children's nonfiction publishing since 1999. Rachel lives on a small desert ranch in Arizona. She enjoys spending time with her family and barnyard of animals. Thanks to our wireless world, her ranch stays tapped into developing technology.